FUTURE TECH

SATELLITES
NOW AND INTO THE FUTURE

Steve Parker

ILLUSTRATED BY INDUSTRIAL ART STUDIO

Belitha Press

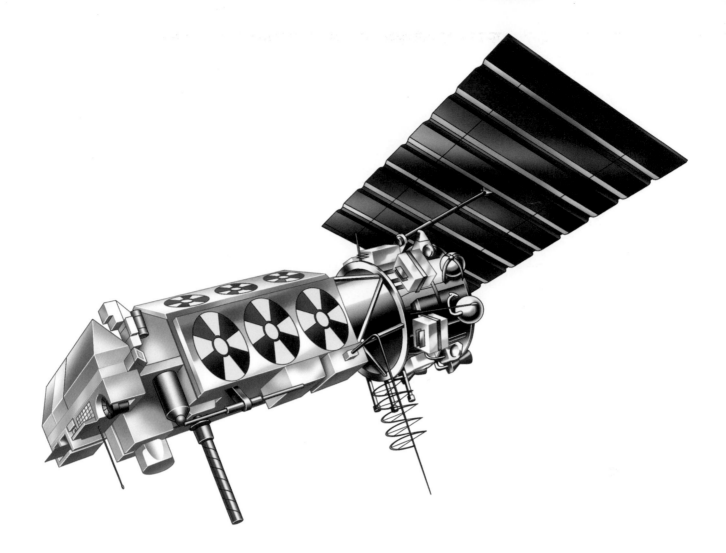

First published in Great Britain in 1998 by

 Belitha Press Limited,
London House, Great Eastern Wharf
Parkgate Road, London SW11 4NQ

Copyright in this format © Belitha Press Limited 1998
Text copyright © Steve Parker 1998

Editor Veronica Ross
Designer Hayley Cove
Illustrations by Industrial Art Studio
Production Paul Harding
Consultants Ian Graham and Virginia Whitby
Picture researcher Diana Morris

ISBN 1 85561 732 3 Hardback
ISBN 1 85561 840 0 Paperback

British Library Cataloguing in Publication Data
for this book is available from the British Library

Printed in Hong Kong / China

Photo credits
Alex Bartel/SPL: 5t. CNES, 1990 Distribution SPOT
Image/SPL: 19l.
Simon Fraser/SPL: 5b.
Gable/Jerrican/SPL:12.
Hen Coop Enterprises/SPL: 9.
INMARSAT/TRH: 16t.
Joyce Lomman/Rex: 27.
Lucasfilm/20th Century Fox/Moviestore: 28.
John Mead/SPL: 7l.
Christopher Morris/Black Star/Colorific!: 25t.
NASA: 19r & front cover. NASA/SPL: 7r, 10, 13, 23t.
Novosti/SPL: 6l, 24t. NRAO/SPL: 22b.
NRSC Ltd/SPL: 21t, 26t.
Rex/Sipa/Zebar: 14.
Space Frontiers/TCL: 20b. Stockmarket: 17b.
Wellcraft Marine: 4bl.
Page 18: artwork based on information from a NASA image.

Words in **bold** appear in the glossary on pages 30-31.

CONTENTS

INTRODUCTION

Satellites are an important part of modern life. We use them every day without realizing it. Tomorrow's weather forecast, news events happening every minute around the world, long-distance phone calls and **Internet** computer connections, are all sent by satellite.

WHAT IS A SATELLITE?

A satellite is an object that goes around, or orbits, something else. For example, the Moon is a natural satellite of the Earth. But when we talk about satellites, we usually mean the artificial or man-made objects that are launched into space to orbit the Earth. Each satellite zooms through dark, silent space hundreds of kilometres above us. But a satellite is far from quiet. It receives thousands of **radio signals** every second from Earth. It also sends thousands of radio signals back to Earth every second.

A speedboat races across the ocean.
The crew know their exact position, by satellite navigation.

FUTURE TREND

Predicting the future is very difficult. A new invention may be in daily use in five years time, or it may be delayed for 30 years. It may never happen at all. What is certain is that technology develops all the time. *Future Trend* looks at new developments, which may happen in 20, 40, or even 60 years. They may seem impossible to us today. But for people 50 years ago, so were satellites.

In the world of big business, dealers make millions as satellite links flash the latest finance news around the globe.

Satellites help to make maps of the Earth's surface, such as the ever-changing ice sheet that covers Antarctica.

WHAT ARE SATELLITES USED FOR?

International industries and businesses exchange billions of items of information every second using satellite links. Spy satellites can photograph military bases, troop movements and missile bases in every corner of the globe. Survey satellites map the land and study its use by farmers, loggers, miners and builders. Navigation satellites help explorers, sailors, pilots and travellers to find their way. And each day, thousands of people buy satellite dishes so that they can watch satellite TV at home. The satellite business is growing fast, and it will become even more important in the future.

A BRIEF HISTORY OF SATELLITES

The Satellite Age began on 4 October 1957 when the **USSR** launched *Sputnik 1* into space. *Sputnik* was a metal ball, 58 centimetres across, weighing 84 kilograms. It orbited Earth every 90 minutes at heights of 220–1000 kilometres. It contained a small radio transmitter, and a thermometer to measure temperatures in space. It seems simple today, but at the time the world was amazed. *Sputnik 1* sent back radio signals to Earth, but after about 90 days, it fell back into the Earth's atmosphere, and burned up as a **shooting star**.

EARLY SATELLITES

In January 1958 the USA launched its first satellite, *Explorer 1*. It carried several scientific instruments and sent back information about **rays** and **radiation** in space. Early satellites were used mainly for scientific research, to find out about conditions in space, and to look at distant stars and galaxies.

The first satellite, *Sputnik 1*, had a ball-shaped case with radio equipment inside.

▷ FUTURE TREND

SATELLITE SMASH-UP?
About 15 000 objects orbit the Earth. They include satellites, bits of old rockets, as well as natural lumps of rock called meteorites. The chances of collision are small, but growing all the time. Rockets and satellites are launched with different orbits so they should avoid each other, but accidents happen. An object smaller than a golf ball could smash a satellite worth $100 million into thousands of tiny pieces.

 All satellites, like this *Intelsat IV* from the 1970s, have many tests before launch.

SATELLITES IN DAILY LIFE

Satellites began to affect daily life in 1962 with the launch of *Telstar*. It sent live television pictures across the Atlantic, between the USA and Europe. But *Telstar* could only work for short periods because of its type of orbit. In 1965, another communications satellite was launched. 'Early Bird' or *Intelsat I* had a different orbit which allowed it to be used all the time. It marked the start of the worldwide satellite communications network.

MORE SATELLITES

Since those early days, more than 4000 satellites have been launched. Over half are no longer in use. Some have drifted away into space, or fallen back to Earth and burned up. Others are still in orbit, but switched off or without power. Today, at least one satellite is launched every week.

 Terrestrial (ground-based) radio and television signals are broadcast from very tall masts.

HOW A SATELLITE WORKS

A satellite is one of the most expensive pieces of machinery in the world. Making its parts small and light make it less costly to launch. But a satellite must be able to withstand the freezing cold temperatures when it is in Earth's shadow, and the great heat of the Sun.

Cube design

SHAPES AND SIZES

There are two main designs of satellites. One is the cylinder or drum. These types of satellite are from one to five metres long. The casing is coated on the outside with shiny **solar panels**, which turn sunlight into electricity. The cube design has solar panels on either side. The standard size of the cube is 1.8 metres, but some larger satellites are as big as a family car.

Drum design

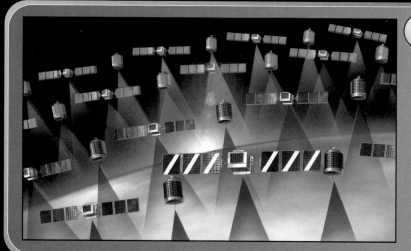

▷ FUTURE TREND

SATELLITE TAKEOVER?
Some sophisticated satellites can communicate with each other in space using radio signals. At the same time, computers are also becoming more intelligent. The Internet brings together millions of computers linked by hundreds of satellites. Could these machines develop their own intelligence, escape from our control and try to take over the world?

UPS AND DOWNS

A typical satellite is controlled by radio signals. These are beamed from a large dish-shaped aerial or **antenna** at the ground station on the Earth's surface. This transfer of information is called the uplink. The satellite beams information about its position, the state of its batteries, photographs or measurements it has taken, and so on, to the same or another ground station. This is called the downlink.

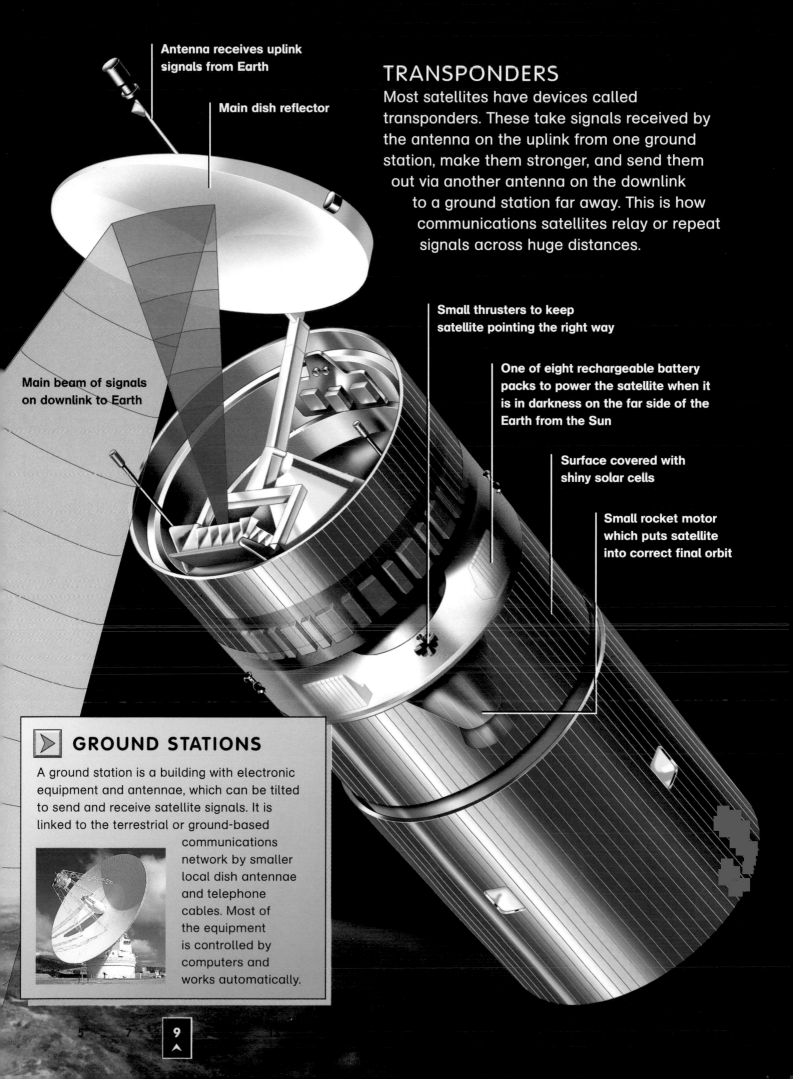

Antenna receives uplink signals from Earth

Main dish reflector

TRANSPONDERS

Most satellites have devices called transponders. These take signals received by the antenna on the uplink from one ground station, make them stronger, and send them out via another antenna on the downlink to a ground station far away. This is how communications satellites relay or repeat signals across huge distances.

Main beam of signals on downlink to Earth

Small thrusters to keep satellite pointing the right way

One of eight rechargeable battery packs to power the satellite when it is in darkness on the far side of the Earth from the Sun

Surface covered with shiny solar cells

Small rocket motor which puts satellite into correct final orbit

▷ GROUND STATIONS

A ground station is a building with electronic equipment and antennae, which can be tilted to send and receive satellite signals. It is linked to the terrestrial or ground-based communications network by smaller local dish antennae and telephone cables. Most of the equipment is controlled by computers and works automatically.

LAUNCHING A SATELLITE

Most satellites are launched into orbit by rockets called ELVs (expendable launch vehicles). The rockets include *Atlas*, *Delta* and *Titan* from the USA, *Proton* and *Energiya* from Russia, China's *Long March* series, Japan's *H1* and *H2*, and the European ArianeSpace's *Ariane* series. Rockets are very expensive to build and after they have been launched they burn up or drift away into space. The only reusable launch vehicles are the US Space Shuttles.

FUTURE TREND

SHOOTING SATELLITES?
Rockets are very costly, and apart from the Space Shuttle, they end up as space junk. Are there cheaper ways to launch a satellite? One way might be to fire the satellite into space using a giant gun. The gun would need a barrel at least two kilometres long. But the gun could not launch a manned spacecraft. The **g-force** of acceleration as it left the barrel would flatten the astronauts!

IN ORBIT

How does a satellite stay in orbit? Any object travels in a straight line unless a force, such as **gravity**, pulls on it. A satellite tries to go in a straight line, but Earth's gravity pulls it down. The satellite falls towards Earth, but it never gets there because the Earth's surface is curved around and away from the satellite. The satellite follows the curve, and in this way continually circles the Earth.

The US Space Shuttle *Atlantis* blasts off from the Kennedy Space Centre, USA.

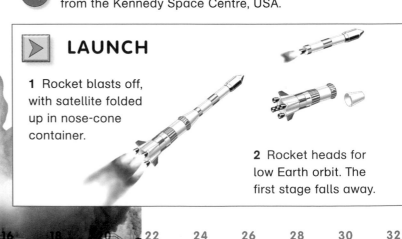

LAUNCH

1 Rocket blasts off, with satellite folded up in nose-cone container.

2 Rocket heads for low Earth orbit. The first stage falls away.

SATELLITE ORBITS

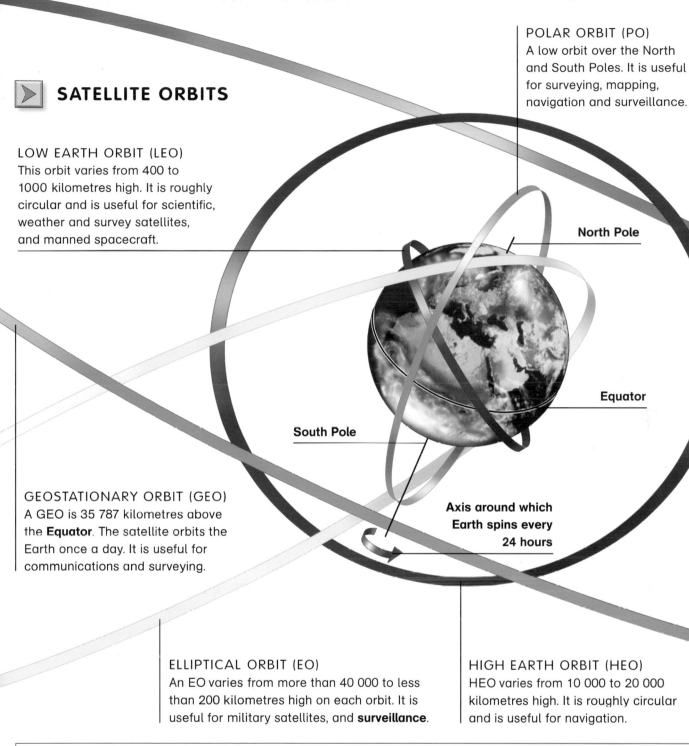

POLAR ORBIT (PO)
A low orbit over the North and South Poles. It is useful for surveying, mapping, navigation and surveillance.

LOW EARTH ORBIT (LEO)
This orbit varies from 400 to 1000 kilometres high. It is roughly circular and is useful for scientific, weather and survey satellites, and manned spacecraft.

North Pole

Equator

South Pole

GEOSTATIONARY ORBIT (GEO)
A GEO is 35 787 kilometres above the **Equator**. The satellite orbits the Earth once a day. It is useful for communications and surveying.

Axis around which Earth spins every 24 hours

ELLIPTICAL ORBIT (EO)
An EO varies from more than 40 000 to less than 200 kilometres high on each orbit. It is useful for military satellites, and **surveillance**.

HIGH EARTH ORBIT (HEO)
HEO varies from 10 000 to 20 000 kilometres high. It is roughly circular and is useful for navigation.

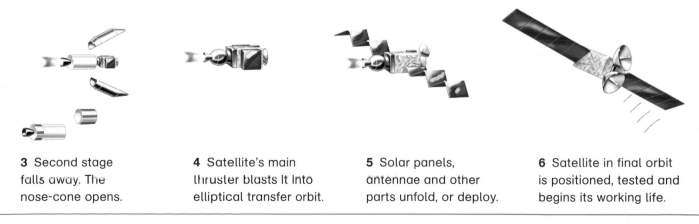

3 Second stage falls away. The nose-cone opens.

4 Satellite's main thruster blasts it into elliptical transfer orbit.

5 Solar panels, antennae and other parts unfold, or deploy.

6 Satellite in final orbit is positioned, tested and begins its working life.

THE COMSAT EXPLOSION

There are hundreds of comsats (communications satellites) in orbit around the Earth. The comsat passes, repeats or relays radio signals between places on the ground that may be thousands of kilometres apart. The signals can represent almost anything, including people talking on the telephone, signals from fax machines, computers, **e-mail**, and the Internet.

The Internet uses satellites to pass on, or relay, radio signals for the words and pictures on a computer screen.

BUSINESSES AND BANKS

Comsats also broadcast radio and TV programmes, and send information to international banks and businesses. A modern comsat can handle 30 000 telephone calls and five colour TV channels at the same time.

SENDING OUT SIGNALS

When you talk into a phone, or send a fax, the sounds of your voice or the marks on the paper are changed to electrical signals. In the telecom network, the signals are changed into very fast on-off bleeps of **digital** code. These bleeps are sent around the network, and bleeped up to a satellite as digital radio signals. The signals are bleeped back to Earth, where the process is reversed, so that the person you are speaking to on the phone can hear your voice.

▷ FUTURE TREND

STEALING SATELLITE SECRETS?
Comsats pass on enormous amounts of secret information, such as government defence plans, or new inventions. This can be sent in coded form by a narrow downlink beam to one small receiving dish, so that other people cannot listen in. But criminals could use a high flying plane or a reflector dish on a tall mast to intercept the signals. They would break the code and sell the secret information for huge sums of money.

GEOSTATIONARY ORBIT

Most comsats are in geostationary or geosynchronous orbit (GEO). The satellites speed along at 11 700 km/h, but from the Earth, they seem to hang perfectly still in the sky. The satellite is available all the time, and antenna dishes can be left pointing at it.

COMSAT SYSTEMS

Comsat systems began with Intelsat, the international telecommunications satellite organization, named in 1965. About 135 nations now belong to Intelsat. They pay for a worldwide system of 20 comsats. Global events screened live on TV, such as the Olympic Games, usually come via Intelsat.

 This *Intelsat VI* comsat, in low earth orbit, will soon boost into the much higher geostationary orbit.

REACHING ALL AREAS

Comsat systems are especially useful for very large countries, or those with remote and mountainous areas, or with lots of scattered islands. These features make it difficult to send signals in the usual way, by terrestrial radio (at the surface) or along cables.

 WORLDWIDE COMSATS

 EUTELSAT
Set up by the European Space Agency to serve Europe, from Iceland to Turkey.

 AUSSAT
Three older and two newer comsats link the whole continent of Australia.

 BRAZILSAT
Dense rainforests and swampy areas make satellites very useful in Brazil.

 INSAT
India is covered by Insat, which also monitors monsoons.

 PHILIPPINES
The Philippines is a nation of islands – perfect for comsats.

 ASIASAT
Centred in China, this system should eventually serve 30 countries and almost half the world's people.

TV SATELLITES

Most satellites communicate only with one or a few ground stations on the Earth's surface. The ground stations have very large dish antennae, 18 metres or more across. Large dishes can pick up very weak signals that cannot be picked up by a domestic satellite TV dish. If the signals are for radio and television programmes, they can be sent from the ground station to local TV and radio centres, and then broadcast from masts or along cables. This is how satellites beam TV pictures from around the world for broadcast on terrestrial TV channels.

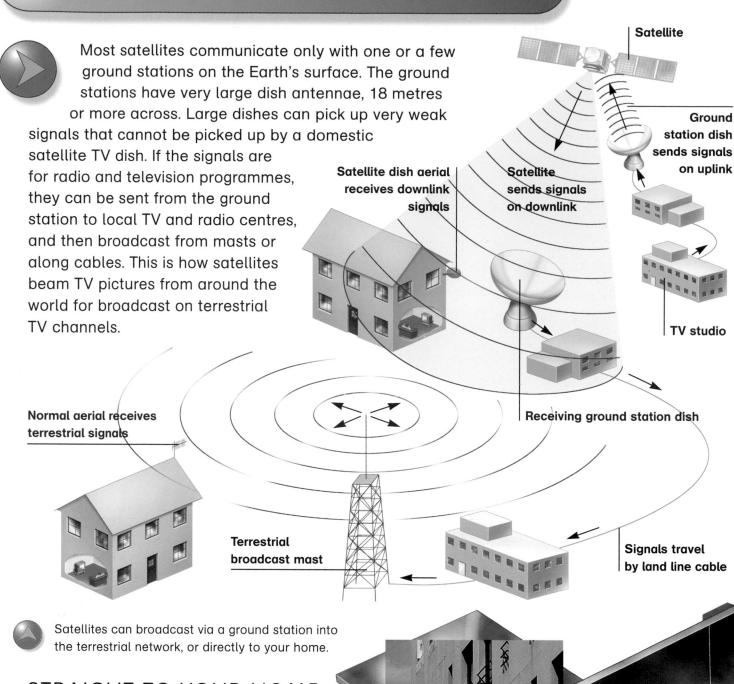

Satellite

Ground station dish sends signals on uplink

Satellite dish aerial receives downlink signals

Satellite sends signals on downlink

TV studio

Normal aerial receives terrestrial signals

Receiving ground station dish

Terrestrial broadcast mast

Signals travel by land line cable

Satellites can broadcast via a ground station into the terrestrial network, or directly to your home.

STRAIGHT TO YOUR HOME

Since the early 1980s, satellites have beamed television and radio signals direct to our homes. This is called DBS (direct broadcasting by satellite). At first, there were two problems to overcome. The signals had to cover a very wide area, so that lots of people could receive them. And, the signals needed to be fairly powerful, so that only a small, cheap satellite dish was needed, plus a **decoder** to attach to the TV set.

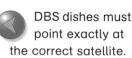

DBS dishes must point exactly at the correct satellite.

MORE AND MORE CHANNELS

During the 1990s new forms of satellite solar cells, batteries, transponders and other equipment were developed. This meant that satellites could broadcast more powerful signals, more widely. The *Hot Bird* series of DBS satellites in Europe, launched in 1996, will give people more satellite TV channels across more of Europe. Japan, Southeast Asia and South America are also developing satellite TV systems.

In the USA, there are already dozens of national channels and hundreds of local ones, available by terrestrial broadcast or cable. So DBS has been slow to start there, but it may soon catch up.

Hot Bird 2

▷ FUTURE TREND

SAT HAT?
Ground stations used to be large buildings with giant dish antennae. Modern portable ground stations can fit into a car or even a suitcase. The user unfolds the dish antenna, points it at the satellite and begins the link. In future, this equipment may be built into a headset, so that anyone, anywhere, could contact the world using a satellite hat.

▷ THE FOOTPRINT

The area over which a satellite broadcasts TV signals is called its footprint. It can be drawn on a map as a number of lines. In the centre, the signals are strongest, so the TV picture and sound are best. Nearer the edge, the signals are weaker, so the picture and sound quality are not so good. The quality can be improved by using a bigger receiver dish to collect more signals.

NAVIGATING BY SATELLITE

Travellers, sailors and explorers used to find their way using a compass, and by measuring the positions of the Sun, Moon and stars. Today, all you need is a GPS (Global Positioning System) receiver. It looks like a mobile phone. When it is switched on, it can tell you where you are anywhere in the world. It will give you a map reference, to the nearest 50 metres or less. It also shows your height above sea level, and if you are moving, how fast you're going and in which direction.

GPS SATELLITES

Today, most planes and ships use satellites to help them navigate. GPS has 24 NAVSTARs (Navigation Satellites for Time and Ranging) in six groups of four. The four members of a group follow each other in one endless orbit, 20 180 kilometres high. The orbits of the six groups are at angles to each other so that the whole world is covered. This means that a ship in the middle of the ocean can pinpoint its exact location.

Even in remote and lonely places, a satellite can link your phone call into the world network.

Future cars with GPS receivers could find their own way and display the route on screen.

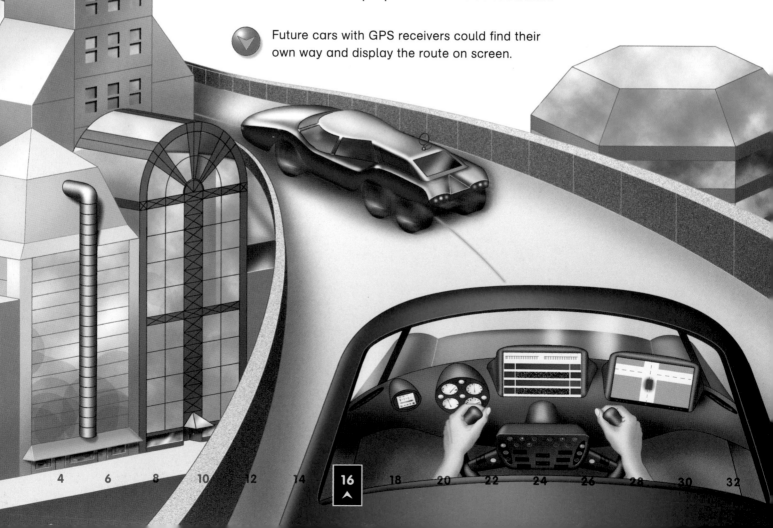

RECEIVING INFORMATION

A GPS receiver on a boat, ship or inside a vehicle anywhere in the world has between six and eleven NAVSTAR satellites passing overhead at any time. The receiver detects their signals, including the code name of the satellite and the exact time, correct to millionths of a second. It takes a different length of time for the signals to travel from each satellite, so the signals from the satellite which is furthest away arrive last. A tiny computer in the receiver takes in the information, and works out where you are.

▷ **FUTURE TREND**

THE IRIDIUM PROJECT?

The Iridium Project plans to put 66 satellites into low earth orbit (LEO). The satellites could be reached by low-power transmitter-receivers, and even mobile telephones, because they would be so close to the Earth. At present mobile phone networks do not stretch very far. In the future it may be possible to use a mobile phone as small as a wristwatch to make a call from the biggest city to the middle of nowhere, via satellites.

A boat and its crew in danger on stormy seas can be located by satellite and rescued by emergency services.

▷ SARSAT

Many planes, boats and vehicles carry a SARSAT transmitter. In an emergency, this sends out radio signals which are detected by a world system of SARSATs, search and rescue satellites. These pick up the emergency message and send their own signals warning of the problem and its location.

SATELLITE SURVEYS

When people travel to a new area, they usually take a map. Survey satellites help to make maps. They have very powerful cameras, which can see fields, roads and buildings, and natural features such as hills, cliffs, rivers and lakes. They also see the sea, with its coasts, islands, ports and ships. The cameras turn the patterns of **light rays** that are given off from everything on the Earth's surface, into radio signals, and beam them down to ground stations on Earth. Here, the radio signals are changed into photographs. These are used to make new maps and check existing ones.

LANDSAT AND SPOT

The main series of survey satellites began in 1972 with *Landsat 1*. Today, *Landsats 4* and *5* go around the Earth 15 times every day. As the Earth spins beneath them, the satellites gradually pass over its surface, detecting images as they go. *SPOT* is a European survey satellite. It orbits about 830 kilometres high and sees a path 20 kilometres wide. It covers the whole planet every 26 days.

▷ WHAT LANDSAT SEES

 As each Landsat orbits, its cameras see a path about 185 kilometres wide.

 The cameras can pick out objects as small as 33 metres wide. So a big building or ship is easily visible.

 Landsat cameras detect ordinary light rays, and also **infra-red** or 'warmth' rays that show up at night.

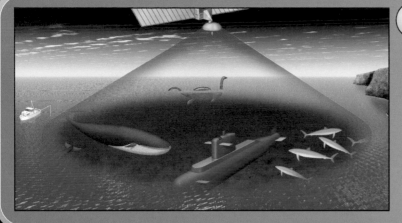

▷ FUTURE TREND

SEEING UNDER THE SEA?
Today's satellites cannot see properly into water to reveal what's below the surface. But one day, someone may invent a type of satellite ray or beam that can pass through water and detect what is in lakes and oceans. The satellite could map the sea-bed, follow shoals of fish and great whales, expose secret submarines, and open up the last great unexplored region on Earth.

EARTH RESOURCES

Photographs from survey satellites show areas of different plants, such as a forest of pine trees and fields of wheat or corn. They can even reveal whether the plants are growing well. This helps farmers to improve their crop yields.

REMOTE SENSING

Survey photos show rock formations and fault lines (cracks) in the ground, which may have reserves of coal, oil or other valuable minerals beneath. This gathering of information from a distance is called remote sensing. Some photos show narrow valleys with fast rivers where dams might be built to produce **hydro-electricity**.

△ A photograph of infra-red 'warmth' rays shows plants as red and the sea as almost black. This is Jakarta, capital of Java.

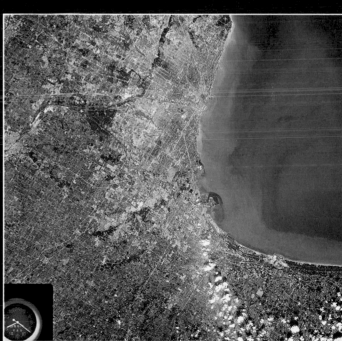

△ The grid-like road network shows clearly in this satellite photo of Chicago, USA.

WHAT'S THE WEATHER LIKE?

Satellites have greatly increased our knowledge of weather and climate, and made our forecasts more accurate. Millions of people rely on daily weather reports, from farmers and fishermen, to the captains of planes and boats.

BEWARE THE HURRICANE

Many series of weather satellites have monitored weather and climate. They began with the first *TIROS* (*Television and Infra-Red Observation Satellite*) in 1960. It recorded cloud cover and different types of clouds, and helped give early warnings of storms such as hurricanes.

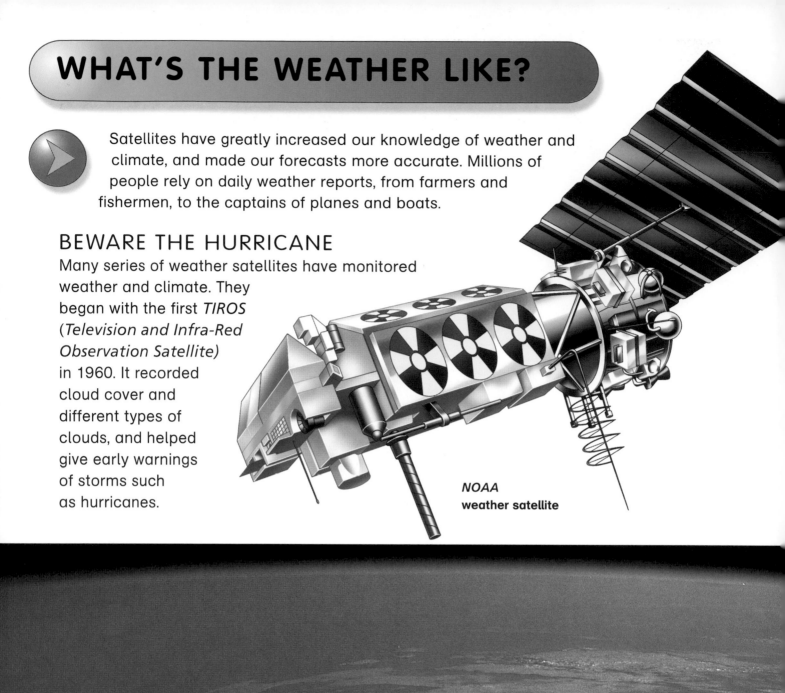

NOAA
weather satellite

A spiral of clouds over the North Atlantic means wet and windy weather for Europe. Britain and France are at the bottom right.

THE OZONE HOLE

Weather satellites show that the world's atmosphere and climate are changing. The *TOMS-Meteor-3* satellite, launched in 1991, monitors the **ozone hole** that appears above the South Pole each spring. If the hole widens and spreads over inhabited lands, it may let through more of the Sun's **ultra-violet** rays. These may harm people, animals and plants on the Earth below.

NOAA REPORTS

From 1970, US *NOAA* satellites (National Oceanographic and Atmospheric Administration) went into polar orbits and monitored the Earth twice every day. Their scientific instruments detect cloud types and cover, snow and ice on the ground, icebergs at sea, the temperature of the air, the temperatures of the ground and sea surface, and humidity – the amount of water vapour in the air.

THE WEATHER NETWORK

There are several weather satellites in geostationary orbit, too. They include Europe's *Meteosats* for Europe and Africa; India's *Insat* for parts of Asia and the Indian Ocean; and the US *GOES* for the east Pacific, North and South America, and the Caribbean. These satellites are linked into a network that monitors the planet's atmosphere, air pressure, winds, temperatures and other information about the weather.

Swirling clouds, photographed by a satellite, give early warning of a hurricane heading for North America.

FUTURE TREND

COULD SATELLITES CHANGE THE WEATHER?

Weather satellites work mainly by **radar** – beaming radio signals down to Earth and detecting the echoes. But what if satellites could send out more powerful types of rays? By beaming these to an exact point in a cloud, they could trigger a shower, stop a storm, or start a hurricane.

SCIENCE SATELLITES

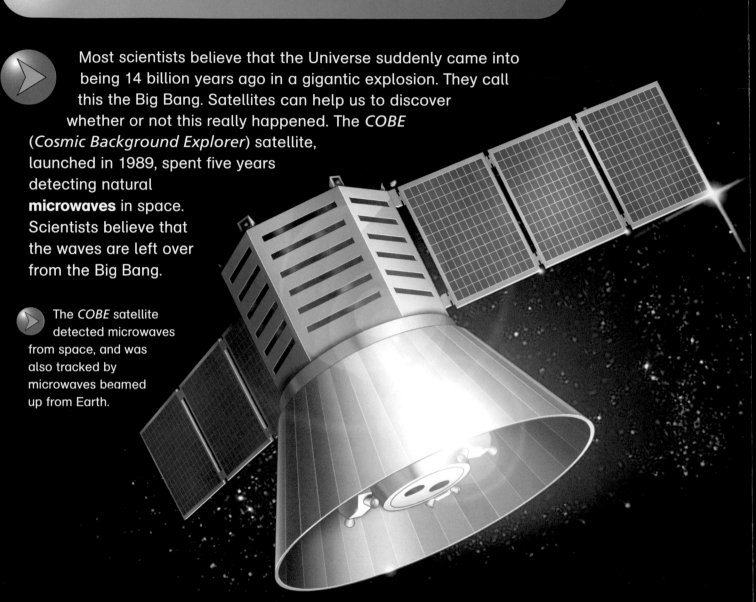

Most scientists believe that the Universe suddenly came into being 14 billion years ago in a gigantic explosion. They call this the Big Bang. Satellites can help us to discover whether or not this really happened. The *COBE* (*Cosmic Background Explorer*) satellite, launched in 1989, spent five years detecting natural **microwaves** in space. Scientists believe that the waves are left over from the Big Bang.

The *COBE* satellite detected microwaves from space, and was also tracked by microwaves beamed up from Earth.

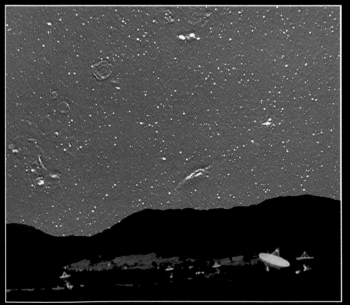

A SKY FULL OF RAYS

When we look at the Moon and stars in the clear night sky, our eyes can only see visible light rays. We cannot see the many other kinds of rays that reach Earth from space. Satellites can. Their instruments detect **radio waves**, infra-red and ultra-violet rays, **x-rays**, **gamma** and **cosmic rays**. They send the information as radio signals to Earth for analysis by scientists.

If your eyes could see radio waves instead of light rays, this is how the night sky might look.

▷ THE HUBBLE SPACE TELESCOPE

One of the biggest satellites was launched by Space Shuttle *Discovery* in 1990. It is the Hubble Space Telescope. It is 13 metres long, 4.3 metres wide, and orbits 613 kilometres high. It's a very powerful telescope, like the ones used on Earth. But it is far above the dust and haze of Earth's atmosphere, so it can see much further and more clearly. After repairs in 1993, it has sent back thousands of fantastic pictures of planets, stars and galaxies.

SOME RECENT FINDINGS

Hundreds of satellites in space are used just for research. The *Compton GRO* (Gamma Ray Observatory) detects gamma rays. It has found 'nurseries' where baby stars are forming from huge clouds of **interstellar dust**. In 1992 the *EUE* (*Extreme Ultra-Violet Explorer*) began to scan the sky for ultra-violet rays. It keeps watch for extremely hot stars which could explode as **supernovas**, and the massive, mysterious objects called **quasars**. *IRAS* (*Infra-Red Astronomy Satellite*) mapped infra-red rays from space. These come mostly from stars that are warming up, but aren't quite hot enough to shine with visible light.

Two Space Shuttle astronauts captured the Hubble Space Telescope for maintenance and improvements, in 1993.

▷ FUTURE TREND

INTERNATIONAL SPACE STATION?
Several countries have planned to build the ISS (International Space Station). The ISS would be the biggest satellite ever, covering the same area as 14 tennis courts. It is due to be flown up in pieces by about 30-40 rockets, and put together in orbit. ISS's main aim is to find out how people can live and work in space in preparation for a manned mission to Mars.

SPY SATELLITES

In the 1950s and 1960s, the USA and the USSR were engaged in a political conflict which became known as the **Cold War**. It was a time of possible **nuclear attack**. In 1963 the Americans launched a series of satellites called *Vela Hotel*, or 'watchman'. They carried instruments which were designed to watch for large explosions and especially tests of nuclear weapons. At the same time, the Russians began building their long-running *Cosmos* series of satellites, to listen into radio messages around the world.

SECRET SATELLITES

Since then, many countries have launched hundreds of satellites to spy on other nations and keep checks on troops, tanks, missile bases, air force planes and navy ships. These satellites are kept secret. The experts who design and operate them do not want ordinary people, and especially other countries, to know what their satellites can see and do. Some countries deny that the satellites exist, or call them observation satellites.

Photographs of Russian *Cosmos* satellites were only released many years after the satellites had fallen out of use.

Individual tanks can be seen by spy satellites far above, which beam the pictures to secret ground stations on Earth.

TYPES OF MILITARY SATELLITES

Most spy satellites are in elliptical or low earth orbit (see page 11), where they can see or hear more. Some have amazingly powerful telescopes that take detailed photographs. These reveal the numbers of troops on a march, the markings on a truck or plane, and even the small round shapes in the ground which are underground missiles. Navigation satellites and the GPS (see page 16) are also used by armies, who must make sure they attack the correct enemy.

CODE-BREAKERS

Some communications satellites are just for military use. They relay secret coded messages between planes, ships, submarines, ground bases and command centres. Other countries use satellites called 'ferrets' to listen into these signals, hoping to break the codes.

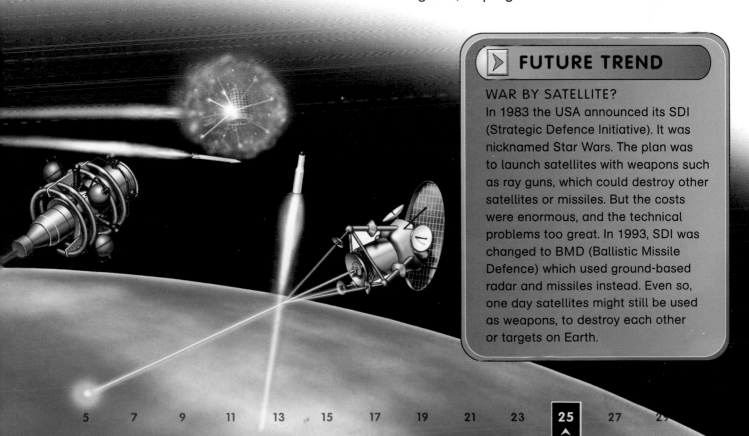

▷ FUTURE TREND

WAR BY SATELLITE?
In 1983 the USA announced its SDI (Strategic Defence Initiative). It was nicknamed Star Wars. The plan was to launch satellites with weapons such as ray guns, which could destroy other satellites or missiles. But the costs were enormous, and the technical problems too great. In 1993, SDI was changed to BMD (Ballistic Missile Defence) which used ground-based radar and missiles instead. Even so, one day satellites might still be used as weapons, to destroy each other or targets on Earth.

THE SATELLITE POLICE

Spy satellites are used to help countries snoop on each other, and check their latest troop movements or missile bases. But the images and information from these satellites can be used for many other law-and-order purposes, where countries work together to fight international problems, such as pollution and drug smuggling. Here are four ways in which satellites might be used.

RAINFOREST PROTECTION

A group of people begin to cut down trees in a rainforest. The area is a protected nature park, and cutting down trees is illegal. Satellite pictures show the growing hole in the forest, and smoke from burning twigs and leaves. Wildlife rangers and police are soon on the scene to stop the damage and arrest the people.

 Computer-coloured satellite photos show how Brazil's natural rainforests (dark green) are logged and cleared in strips, for timber and farmland.

▷ FUTURE TREND

SATELLITE KIDNAP?
There are several ways that criminals or terrorists might kidnap a satellite. They could jam the control signals so that the satellite drifts into space and becomes useless. They might send secret control signals to the satellite's computer systems which would run the batteries down so low that the satellite no longer works. Or another spacecraft could capture the orbiting satellite, even knocking it out of its orbit.

TRACKING THE SHIPMENT

Drug squad police suspect that a boat is being used to smuggle drugs into a country. One night, the police secretly attach a radio beacon to the boat. This shows the boat's position by satellite navigation, and sends the information as radio signals to the police. Even at night, they can track the boat's exact movements, and catch the drug smugglers.

A radio 'bug' on this boat, tracked by satellite, helps to prove that it carries illegal drugs.

WATER SHORTAGE

No rain has fallen for months. Farmers are told that they cannot water their crops, unless they have a special licence. In satellite photographs, one farmer's fields look amazingly green, but a nearby small lake has shrunk. The water authorities discover that the farmer has been pumping water illegally from the lake on to his fields.

CATCHING THE TERRORISTS

A satellite detects radio signals coming from a tall aerial in the middle of a desert. The signals are on an unusual channel, and in a strange code. Computer engineers break the code, and discover a terrorist plot to threaten world peace. The national army soon discover the terrorists' underground base in the desert, and stop the plot.

SATELLITES AND SETI

Many research satellites orbiting the Earth detect rays and signals coming from deep space. Computers study these signals for certain features, such as regular stops and starts, changes in strength, or other repeated patterns. This might indicate that the signals are not natural. They could come from aliens. This is called SETI (the Search for Extra-Terrestrial Intelligence).

IS ANYONE OUT THERE?

Today's real SETI programme listens to some types of radio signals using ground stations. It also sends out messages into the Universe in the hope that someone or something is listening.

MYSTERIOUS MESSAGES

A big SETI satellite in orbit far above the Earth could detect much weaker signals from space, away from the atmosphere and the busy air waves around Earth. It might be able to pick up other forms of messages, such as patterns of mysterious **gravitational waves**. But it would be very expensive to build the satellite, launch it into space, and pay for people to study the signals.

Space could be teeming with fun places to go and interesting aliens to meet.

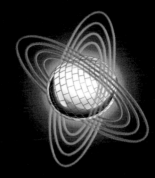

WHO WOULD KNOW?

What if signals really were received from aliens? Unless the aliens could travel through space, they would be at home – billions of kilometres away. Even radio signals, which go at the speed of light, would take years to travel such distances. One of our spacecraft would take centuries.

ALIEN VISITORS

But if the aliens could travel through space, then they might be closer than we'd like. They would also be more advanced, in machinery and technology, than we are. They might view humans as amusing creatures, like pets. Or they might think that we were nasty, aggressive beings who were destroying our world. To save the planet, the aliens might get rid of us!

▷ FUTURE TREND

TAKE ME TO YOUR LEADER?
Aliens on the way to Earth might pick up the huge numbers of radio signals being sent around by satellites, long before they get here. They could find and meet a satellite in geostationary orbit, while they were still 35 000 kilometres away from the Earth. They might think that this satellite is on guard, protecting its planet, and that all the beings on Earth look just like it. To them, Earth might be a world full of satellites.

GLOSSARY

antenna An antenna can be a straight or looped wire, a bar with side arms (like a TV aerial), a disc, bowl or dish. It sends out or receives radio and similar signals, and is sometimes called an aerial.

Cold War A time during the 1950s, 60s and 70s when the USA and its Western allies, and the USSR and its Eastern allies, were suspicious of each other. Both sides built up powerful armed forces and threatened nuclear attack.

cosmic rays Beams of very tiny particles, such as parts of atoms, that pass through space in all directions. They may come from massive exploding stars and other objects.

decoder A device that converts radio, electrical or other signals from one coded form, such as digital code (see below), into other coded forms that can be used by other equipment, such as television sets.

digital Using digits or whole numbers, such as 1, 2, 3 and so on. Information such as words and pictures can be put into digital code for sending by radio waves or as electrical pulses along wires.

e-mail Electronic mail – words, pictures and other information sent along wires or by radio signals, usually between computers. It goes from sender to receiver almost instantly.

Equator The imaginary line around the middle of the Earth at its widest part, midway between the North and South Poles.

g-force A way of measuring forces based on g, the downward pull of Earth's gravity. We can feel changes in g-force during roller coaster rides.

gamma rays Rays or waves which are part of the electromagnetic spectrum, EMS. (See **light rays**.) They are similar to light and x-rays, but have shorter waves. They are made by nuclear reactions and radioactive substances, and also come from space.

gravitational waves Rays or waves that may carry the pulling effects of gravity. They have never actually been detected.

gravity The natural pulling force between any two objects. Bigger objects have more gravitational pull. Earth's gravity keeps us pulled down on to its surface.

hydro-electricity Electricity made from the energy of flowing water, usually by building a dam across a river and using the water to turn turbine-generators.

infra-red Rays or waves which are part of the electromagnetic spectrum, EMS. (See **light rays**.) They are similar to visible light rays, but have waves slightly longer than those of visible red light. We cannot see infra-red rays, but we can feel them as they can have a warming or heating effect.

Internet The worldwide network or web of computers and similar electronic machines, linked by the wires, cables and satellites of the telephone system.

interstellar dust Various tiny particles that drift about in space. Interstellar means between the stars.

light rays Rays or waves which are part of the electromagnetic spectrum, EMS. Light rays can be detected by our eyes. The rays range in colour from red through green to blue and violet, the colours of the light spectrum. (The EMS includes radio waves, ultra-violet rays, infra-red rays, X-rays, gamma rays. The rays of the EMS are types of energy that travel like waves. They differ in the size of their wavelengths.)

microwaves Rays or waves which are part of the electromagnetic spectrum, EMS. (See **light rays**.) They are similar to radio and light rays, and their waves are about 1 to 100 centimetres long. We cannot see them, but we can use them to make heat.

nuclear attack Warfare using nuclear or atomic weapons such as bombs or missiles, which would cause great destruction, and widespread pollution.

ozone hole A thinner than normal area of the ozone layer around the Earth, caused mainly by pollution with man-made chemicals.

quasars Incredibly bright and hugely powerful objects deep in space. They may be the centres of newly forming galaxies.

radar A system for detecting objects, such as planes, ships and clouds, by beaming out radio waves that bounce or reflect off the object. The reflections or echoes are analyzed to show the object's direction, distance, and perhaps size and shape. Radar means RAdio Detection And Ranging.

radiation Any form of energy that is given out, or radiated, from a source as rays, waves or particles. It includes the various waves or rays of the electromagnetic spectrum, such as radio waves, microwaves, infra-red rays, light rays, ultra-violet rays and x-rays and particles such as cosmic rays and certain forms of radioactivity.

radio signals Radio waves of varying strengths, or in on-off pulses, which carry information in coded form. The information can include words, pictures, sounds and computer data.

radio waves Rays or waves which are part of the electromagnetic spectrum, EMS. (See **light rays**.) They are similar to microwaves and light rays, but their waves are much longer, from one metre to many kilometres.

rays A form of energy that can be sent out as beams or waves – see radiation.

shooting star A meteor (lump of rock), rocket part, old satellite or similar object in space, that comes back very fast into the air of the Earth's atmosphere, heats up and burns with a fiery streak of light.

solar panels Panels that contain many smaller solar cells. These are electronic devices that convert light energy (usually solar light from the Sun) into electricity.

supernova A star which becomes so big and bright that it explodes, like a huge fireball deep in space.

surveillance Gathering information about a person, organization or country.

terrestrial Based on Earth or very near the Earth's surface.

ultra-violet Rays or waves which are part of the electromagnetic spectrum, EMS. (See **light rays**.) They are similar to light rays, but their waves are shorter. We cannot see ultra-violet rays, but they are responsible for tanning our skins in the summer. Too much ultra-violet light can be harmful and cause burning.

USSR Union of Soviet Socialist Republics (Soviet Union), a group of states in Eastern Europe and Asia which rivalled the USA as a world superpower. It split apart in 1991.

x-rays Rays or waves which are part of the electromagnetic spectrum, EMS. (See **light rays**.) They are similar to radio and light rays, but their waves are very short, with millions packed into one centimetre. They can pass through soft substances such as flesh and wood, but not through dense substances such as bone and many metals. X-rays can harm living things even in small amounts.

INDEX